KEY STAGE 3 MATHEMATICS Paper 1/2

PRACTICE TEST 21

Time :
Total time for this test is 1 hour.

Instructions :
Write your name in the space below.
Write your answers in the spaces
provided in the paper.
Check your work carefully.

Information :
Total mark for this Test is 66.
Numbers in brackets at the end of
each question indicate the marks awarded
to each answer or part of an answer.

Mark	
Total	66 (Maximum)

Pupil Name :
_____

1.   Sally has three £1 coins, five 50p coins and seven 20p coins.

a.   How much money has she altogether ?

Answer £ _____   [1]

b.   A Video tape costs £7 . 99. How much more money does Sally need in order to buy one tape ?

Answer £ _____   [1]

c.   Sally has a big collection of Video tapes.

She has the shelf, shown below, made.

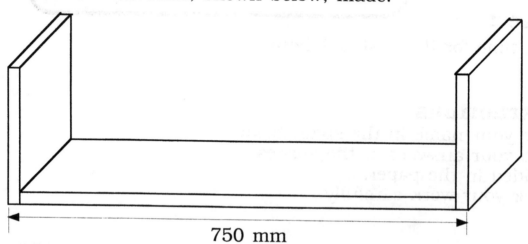

750 mm

The shelf is 750 mm long while the thickness of a tape is 25 mm.

How many tapes will the shelf hold ?

Answer _____ tapes   [2]

d.   If Sally has 240 tapes how many similar shelves does she need to hold her collection of tapes ?

Answer _____ shelves   [2]

2. In the foyer of a cinema the Prices were displayed as shown. A family of three children (ages 6, 10 and 14) and two parents went to the cinema.

CINEMAPLEX

ADULTS.....................£12.00

CHILDREN (under16)...£ 5.00

What was the total admission price ?

Answer £ _____ [2]

3. A calendar for December 2001 is shown below.

December 2001						
Mon	Tue	Wed	Thu	Fri	Sat	Sun
				1	2	
3	4	5	6	7	8	9
10	11	12	13	14	15	16
17	18	19	20	21	22	23
24	25	26	27	28	29	30
31						

a. On what date was the third Saturday of the month. ?

Answer _____ [1]

b. A flood occurred on November 27th 2001. What day of the week was this ?

Answer _____ [1]

c. John and Ann had their wedding on January 15th 2002. What day of the week was this ?

Answer _____ [2]

3.

4.

Here is a square with sides 4cms long.

4 cms

a. What is the area of this square ?

Answer _____ sq.cms. [1]

b. What is the perimeter of this square ?

Answer _____ cms [1]

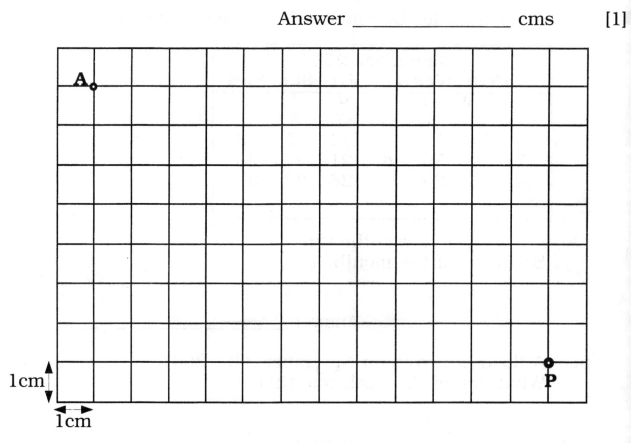

1cm

1cm

c. On this grid draw a rectangle that has the same area as the square above. Start at point **A.** [2]

d. On the grid draw another rectangle that has the same perimeter as the square above. Start at point **P.** [2]

4.

5.   Below is a table showing the rainfall for a week in October.

Sun	Mon	Tues	Wed	Thur	Fri	Sat
6mm	4mm	6mm	10mm	2mm	1mm	6mm

a.   Complete the barchart for the other days of the week.   [2]

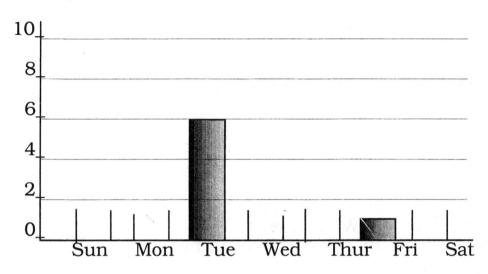

b.   What was the **mean** daily
rainfall for this week ?

Answer _____ mm   [2]

c.   What is the **median** daily rainfall ?

Answer _____ mm   [1]

d.   What is the **modal** daily rainfall ?

Answer _____ mm   [1]

6. 80 pupils from an inner city school went on a day trip to Lough Erne.

64 pupils went by bus while the rest travelled by car.

a. What fraction of the pupils went by bus ?

Answer _____ [1]

b. What percentage of the pupils went by car ?

Answer _____% [1]

c. One of the pupils was chosen for a free shopping trip.What was the probability that this pupil travelled by car ?

Answer _____ [2]

d. The probability that the pupil chosen for the shopping trip was a boy was **1**.

What does this tell you about the pupils who took the day trip to Lough Erne ?

Answer _____

_____ [1]

7. A young bank official earns £1000 per month.

She spends $\frac{1}{5}$ of her salary on her food and clothing, $\frac{2}{5}$ on rent, $\frac{1}{10}$ on entertainment and she saves the remainder .

What fraction of her monthly salary does she save ?

Answer _____ [2]

SHOW ALL YOUR WORKING

The table below shows the cost of music lessons .

	2 lessons	6 lessons	10 lessons
Child	£3.50	£9.00	£14.00
Adult	£6.00	£15.00	£25.00

a.   The Edams family booked a course of 10 lessons for the two parents and two children.

What was the total cost ?

Answer £_____   [2]

b.   The children of another family had 2 lessons each. The total cost for them was £17.50.

How many children were in the family ?

Answer _____ children.   [2]

9.   a.   How many times is the **2** in **25.06** greater than the **2** in the number **34.2** ?

Answer _____   [1]

b.   How many times is the **9** in **4.79** less than the **9** in the number **19.6** ?

Answer _____   [1]

10. A Maths class has invented a number game with number cards.

$$\boxed{2}\ \boxed{3}\ \boxed{4}\ \boxed{5}\ \boxed{6}\ \boxed{7}\ \boxed{8}\ \boxed{9}$$

a. Which TWO cards have SQUARE numbers ?

Answer ◯◯ [1]

b. Use TWO cards to make the biggest fraction less than 1 whole.

[1]

c. Use TWO cards to make a fraction less than $\frac{1}{4}$

[1]

d. Use 4 cards to show TWO fractions that are equivalent to $\frac{1}{3}$

[2]

11. If 11 books cost £13 . 20 how much would 9 similar books cost ?

Answer £ _____ [1]

12. A boat left Port A for a cruise around the sea and back to Port A.

The course which the boat followed is shown on the grid.

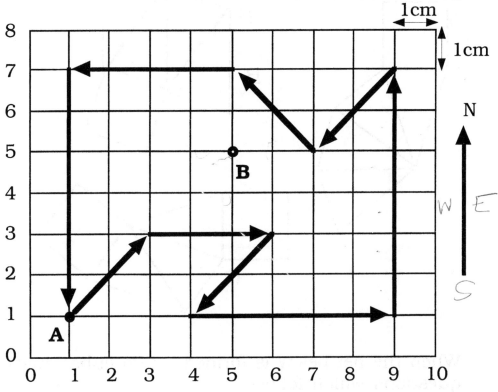

a. Describe the course of the boat using the eight compass points.

The course has been started :- [2]

NE, E, SW, _____, _____, _____, _____, _____, _____

b. If you were travelling from Port B to Port A in what direction would you be travelling ?

Answer _____ [1]

c. What are the co-ordinates of Port B ?

Answer _____ [1]

d. The scale of the grid is 1 cm represents 4.5 Kms. For what distance (in Kms) did the boat cruise when it was cruising due North ?

Answer _____ kms [2]

13. Which one of the drawings below is the net of a Square-based Pyramid ?

Tick the correct box.

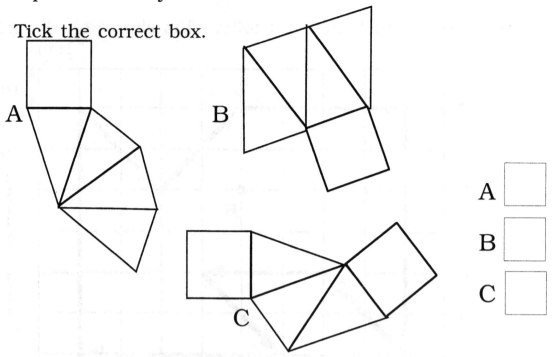

A ☐

B ☐

C ☐

[2]

14. When the net below is formed into a cube answer the questions which follow.

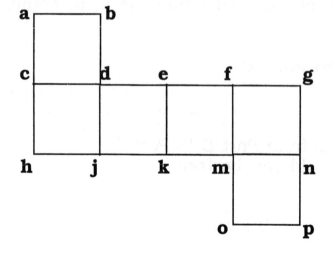

a. Which point will meet **o** ?   Answer _____ [1]

b. Which point will meet **j** ?   Answer _____ [1]

c. Which point will meet **h** ?   Answer _____ [1]

d. Which point will meet **c** ?   Answer _____ [1]

15. a. Plot the following co-ordinates on the grid.

A (0,6)   **B** (8,6)   **C** (10,2)   **D** (2,2)   [1]

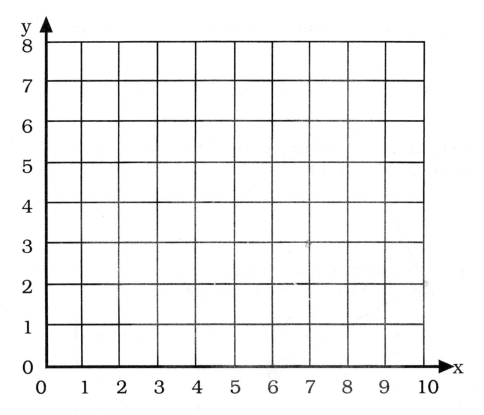

b. When the points are joined
what is the name of the shape ?

Answer _____   [1]

c. What are the co-ordinates of the
centre point of the shape ?

Answer _____   [1]

d. Each square of the grid is 1 cm by 1 cm.
What is the area of this shape ?

Answer _____ sq. cms.   [1]

e. How many lines of symmetry has this shape ?

Answer _____   [1]

16.   Below are the first 3 terms of an algebraic sequence.

y - 1, 2y - 2, 3y - 3, ...

a.   Write down the next 3 terms of this sequence.

Answer _____ , _____ , _____   [1]

b.   Write down in its **simplest form** the **sum** of the first 3 terms. Show your working.

Answer _____   [1]

17.   Match up the pairs of shapes which go together to form exactly the given dotted square.

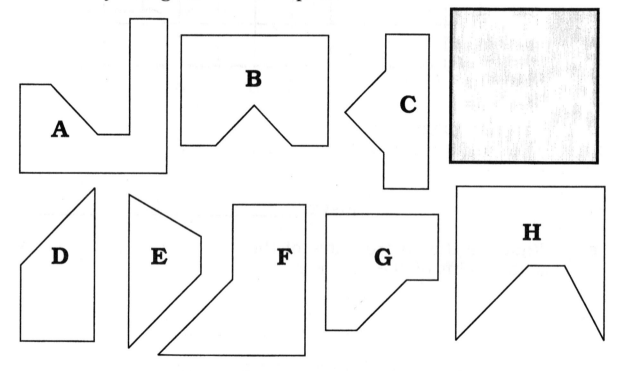

Answers a.   PAIR 1 _____ and _____   [1]

b.   PAIR 2 _____ and _____   [1]

c.   PAIR 3 _____ and _____   [1]

d.   PAIR 4 _____ and _____   [1]

KEY STAGE 3 MATHEMATICS Paper 3

PRACTICE TEST 22

Time :

Total time for this test is 1 hour.

Instructions :

Write your name in the space below.
Write your answers in the spaces
provided in the paper.
Check your work carefully.

Information :

Total mark for this Test is 66.
Numbers in brackets at the end of
each question indicate the marks awarded
to each answer or part of an answer.

Mark	
Total	66 (Maximum)

Pupil Name :

_____

1.   A holiday hotel has 4 floors.
The **First floor** has rooms numbered **10** to **50**.

The **Double Rooms** on this floor have been given door numbers which are **PRIME**.

The **Family Rooms** have **SQUARE** numbers on the doors.

a.   What are the numbers of the **Double Rooms** on the first floor ?

Answer _____   [1]

b.   What are the numbers on the doors of the **Family Rooms** ?

Answer _____   [1]

The **Second Floor** has rooms numbered **61** to **125**.

Two of these rooms are **6-unit Family Rooms** and these are numbered with   **Cubic** numbers .

The **Lounges** on this floor are numbered with numbers which are **Multiples of 12**.

c.   What are the numbers on these large Family rooms ?

Answer _____   [1]

d.   What are the numbers of the Lounges ?

Answer_____   [1]

2.   Simplify the following :-

a.   **2c + 3 x 2d - c**

Answer _____   [1]

b.   **6a² - 2a x 2a**

Answer _____   [1]

3.   This triangular prism has the dimensions shown.
Length = 9 cms, Height = 4 cms and Width = 6 cms.

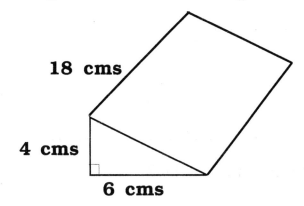

Not drawn to scale.

a.   What is the volume of this solid ?

Answer _____ cubic cms.   [2]

b.   A CUBE has the same volume as this prism.

What is the length of the side of this cube ?

Answer _____ cms.   [2]

4. The drawing is of a Regular Hexagon divided into congruent triangles.

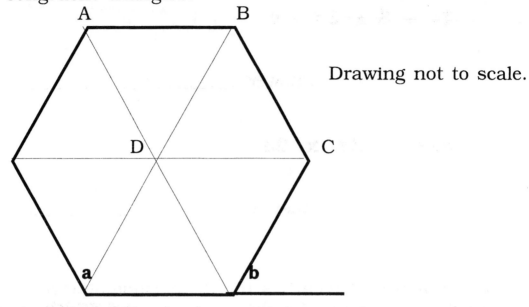

Drawing not to scale.

a. What type of a triangle is ABD ?

Answer _____ [1]

b. What type of a Quadrilateral is ABCD ?

Answer _____ [1]

c. What size is the angle at **a** ?

Answer _____° [2]

d. What size is the angle at **b** ?

Answer _____° [2]

Drawing not to scale.

a.   What type of a triangle is ABD ?

Answer _____   [1]

b.   What type of a Quadrilateral is ABCD ?

Answer _____   [1]

c.   What size is the angle at **a** ?

Answer _____°   [2]

d.   What size is the angle at **b** ?

Answer _____°   [2]

4.

SHOW ALL YOUR WORKING

5. The Spinner below is used in a **"Shape Game"**.

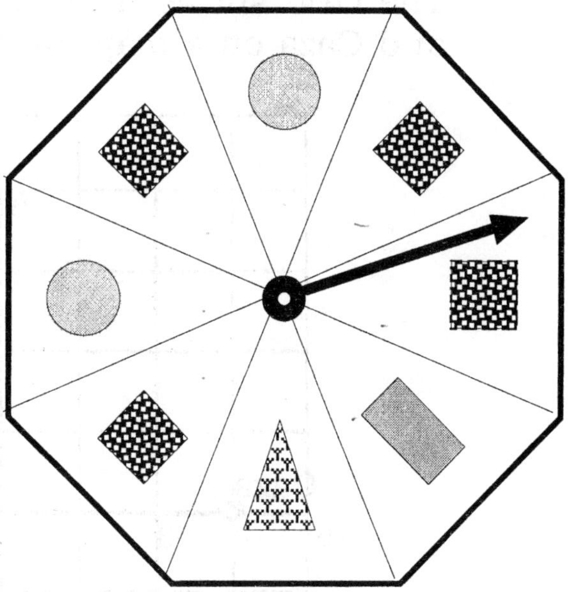

For one spin of the Arrow work out the type of shape it points towards . **The diagram shows a square.**

Write down the shape for each of the following probabilities.

a. The Probability of the Spinner resting on this shape is :-

"one-chance-in-four" .

Answer ______________________________ [1]

b. The Probability of the Spinner resting on this shape is :-

" **50% chance** " .

Answer ______________________________ [1]

c. What is the probability of the spinner resting on a Triangle or a Rectangle ?

Answer ______________________________ [1]

6. The Summer temperature in London is 15°C. There was a difference of 8°C between the London temperature and that of Lisbon.

Write down two possible values for the Summer temperature in Lisbon ?

Answer ________ °C or ________ °C [2]

SHOW ALL YOUR WORKING

7. The Grid shows the positions of three Towns Antel, Brone and Caza on a map, drawn on **1 cm.** squared paper.

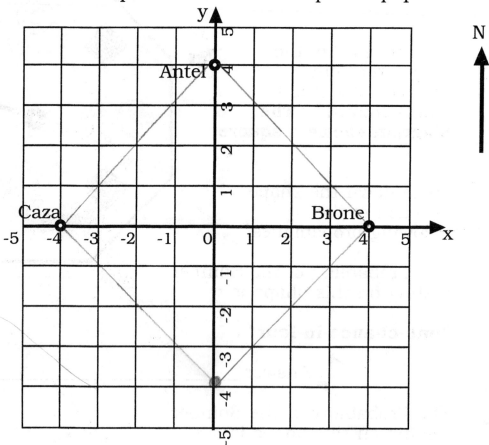

A Fourth town **Drux** will create a square when the 4 towns are joined up.

a. What are the co-ordinates of Drux ?   (____,____)   [2]

b. What are the co-ordinates of Caza ?   (____,____)   [1]

c. If you were to travel from Antel to Brone in which direction would you be travelling ?

Answer _____   [1]

d. If the actual distance from Caza to Brone is 120 Kms what is the scale of the map ?

Answer 1 cm = _____   [2]

6.

8. a. **s** is a square number between 90 and 150.

Write down 3 possible
values of **s**.

Answer _____ [2]

b. **c** is a cubic number between 90 and 150.

Write down the value of **c**.

Answer _____ [2]

c. **m** is a multiple of 11 between 90 and 150.

Write down the 5 values of **m**.

Answer _____ [1]

9. To convert metres to kilometres the rule is **"divide by 1000"**.

metres $\longrightarrow$ ÷ 1000 $\longrightarrow$ kms

a. Convert 33222 metres to kms.

Answer   33222 metres = _____ Kms   [1]

b. Complete the flow diagram below to convert
centimetres to metres.

cms $\longrightarrow$ [   ] $\longrightarrow$ metres

c. Convert 1098 cms to metres.

Answer   1098 cms = _____ metres   [1]

7.

10. An Hotel chef wants to find out the **approximate** numbers of potatoes which weigh 1 Kilogram.

From a bag of potatoes he weighs out 100 grams and counts them. He repeats this **5 times** and records the results as in the table below.

	Number of potatoes
1st 100 g	6
2nd 100 g	4
3rd 100 g	5
4th 100 g	4
5th 100 g	6

a. What is the **best estimate** for the number of potatoes in 100g ?

Answer _____potatoes   [2]

b. Using this estimate how many potatoes should the chef expect to find in 100 Kilograms of potatoes ?

Answer _____potatoes   [2]

c. What would the **approximate** weight be of 750 potatoes ?

Answer _____ kgs.   [1]

11.   Draw the reflection of the following logo in the mirror line AB.

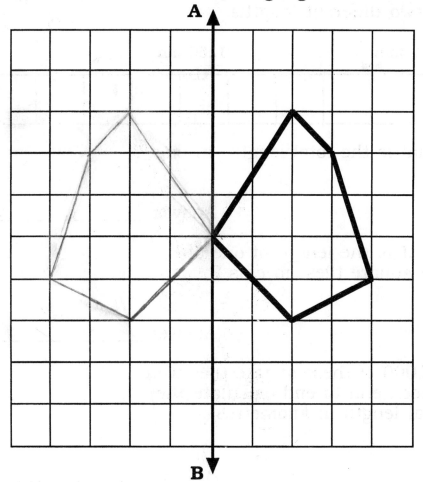

[3]

12.   Find the value of the following.

a.   -7 + 3 x 4

Answer _____   [1]

b.   5 + 3(7 - 3)

Answer _____   [1]

c.   10 - 3 x 3 + 4

Answer _____   [1]

d.   11 - 3(7 - 3)

Answer _____   [1]

13. Below is a drawing of a pattern of border tiles, of two different lengths.

314 mm   1256 mm   314 mm

a. What is the total length in cms ?

Answer _____ cms   [1]

b, What is the length of one of the square tiles in cms ?

Answer _____ cms   [1]

c. If 1000 of these square tiles were placed end to end calculate the total length in kilometres .

Answer _____ kms.   [2]

14. Draw lines to match the expressions on the left with the appropriate expression on the right.

$6a^2$

a. $2a + 4a$

$5a$

$6a$

b. $2a \times 4a$

$9a$

$8aa$

c. $3 \times 3a$

$8a^2$ [3]

10.

15. A plumber uses the following formula for calculating the Price he charges for a job.

$$P = N \times £9 + £15 \text{ (Call-out charge)}$$

P represents **PRICE** and **N** represents the **NUMBER** of work hours.

a. What will the Plumber charge for a job which takes 25 hours to complete ?

Answer £ _____ [1]

b. How many hours does a job last if its total cost is £168 ?

Answer _____ hours [2]

16. Below are some of the capital letters of the alphabet.

E G H Z Q

a. Write down the letter which has **both** Reflective and Rotational symmetry.

Answer_____ [1]

b. Write down the letter which has **only** Reflective symmetry.

Answer _____ [1]

c. Write down the letter which has **only** Rotational symmetry .

Answer_____ [1]

d. Write down the letters which have **neither** Relective **nor** Rotational symmetry.

Answer _____ [1]

SHOW ALL YOUR WORKING

17. The Empire State Building is one of the most popular tourist sights in New York. On a holiday to New York twins Sally and Sean buy souvenirs of the Building.

a. They pay 12 Dollars for each of the models.
The Exchange rate is $1.50 dollars = £1.
What does the model cost in £s ?

Answer £ _____ [1]

b. A model of the Grand Opera House
in Belfast costs £ 9 . 50.
What would it cost in dollars ?

Answer $ _____ [1]

**The model of the Empire State Building
is 18 cm high.**
The scale of the dimensions of
the model is 1 : 1600.

c. What is the actual height of
the building in metres ?
Show your working.

Answer _____ metres

d. The Base of the building is a square, each side 48 metres long.
Using the same scale as above
what is the actual length of the base
in cms. on the model ?

Answer _____ cms [2]

e. The Building itself was built with concrete columns, each 2.4 metres high.

How many columns built end on end were
needed for one row of columns in height ?

Answer _____ columns [2]

12.

KEY STAGE 3 MATHEMATICS Paper 3

PRACTICE TEST 23

Time :
Total time for this test is 1 hour.

Instructions :
Write your name in the space below.
Write your answers in the spaces
provided in the paper.
Check your work carefully.

Information :
Total mark for this Test is 66.
Numbers in brackets at the end of
each question indicate the marks awarded
to each answer or part of an answer.

Mark	
Total	66 (Maximum)

Pupil Name :

_____

1. a. **s** is a square number between 10 and 30.

Write down 2 possible
values of **s**.

Answer _____ [1]

b. **c** is a cubic number between 10 and 30.

Write down the value of **c**.

Answer _____ [1]

c. **m** is a multiple of 7 between 10 and 30.

Write down the 3 values of **m**.

Answer _____ [1]

d. **p** is a prime number
between 10 and 30.

Write down the 6 values of **p**.

Answer _____ [1]

2. John is using the following formula :- $s = ut + \frac{1}{2}at^2$

Find the value of **s** when :-

$$u = 10, \quad a = 3 \quad \text{and} \quad t = -4$$

Answer **s** = _____ [2]

2.

SHOW ALL YOUR WORKING

3. The Giant's Causeway runs a Courtesy bus from the Visitor's Centre to the Causeway itself.

The table below shows the number of passengers on the bus on 11 journeys.

	Number of passengers carried per journey										
Courtesy Bus	15	12	10	17	16	14	11	9	20	17	13

a. What is the Median number of passengers carried per journey ?

Answer _____ [1]

b. What is the Mean number of passengers carried per journey ?

Answer _____ [2]

c. What is the Modal number of passengers carried per journey ?

Answer _____ [1]

4. Draw the reflection of the following logo in the mirror line **AB**.

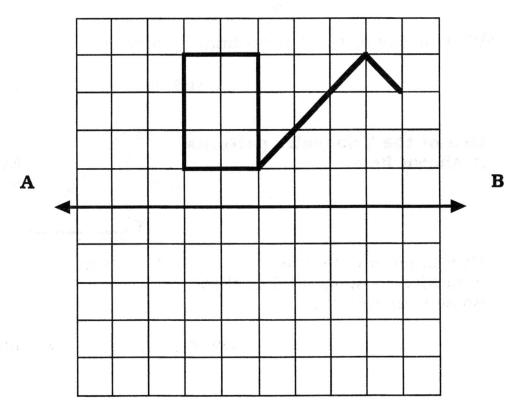

[2]

3.

5.   a.   What is the value of **3c - 2d** if
c = 3 and **d = 5** ?

Answer _____   [1]

b.   What is the value of **2ab + 2cd** if
a = 2, b = 3, c = - 2 and **d = 3** ?

Answer _____   [1]

6.   The Logo below is for a furniture manufacturer and is made
from a wooden square and congruent aluminium triangles.

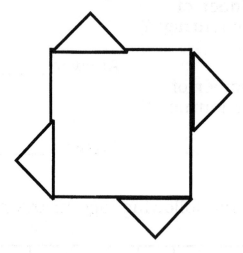

Not drawn to scale.

a.   What is the order of Rotational Symmetry ?

Answer _____   [1]

**One of the Triangular patterns
is shown here.**

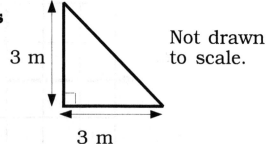

Not drawn
to scale.

3 m

3 m

b.   How much aluminium
is needed to make all 4 of these ?
Show your working.

Answer _____ sq. metres   [2]

7.   Number sequences have the following Rule :-

" Subtract 6 from the previous term !"

a.   Write down the next **THREE** terms in each of the following sequences.

36,   **30,**   _____,   _____,   _____ .   [1]

b.   What is the **PRODUCT** of the
last **2** terms of this sequence ?

Answer _____   [1]

c.   Complete this sequence using the Rule above.

10,   _____,   _____,   _____ .   [1]

d.   What is the **PRODUCT** of the
last **2** terms of this sequence ?

Answer _____   [1]

8.   Of the 60,000 concrete brick produced at a brickworks in a week 2400 had to be rejected as they were faulty.

a.   Calculate the % of bricks which were faulty that week.

Answer _____ %   [2]

b.   The following week 6% of the bricks were rejected.

51,324 bricks were perfect,

What was the total number of bricks produced in this week ?

Answer _____ bricks   [2]

9.   a.   Show that a solution of the equation $3x^2 - 2x = 13$

lies between **x = 2** and **x = 3**.

Show your working.   [2]

b.   Using a trial and improvement method, find the solution to

the equation $3x^2 - 2x = 13$ correct to **1 decimal place**.

Answer **x** = _____   [2]

10.   a.   Calculate the value of :-

$(6 \times 10^{-3}) \times (42 \times 10^{6}) \times (5 \times 10^{4})$

Write your answer in **standard form**.

Answer _____   [2]

b.   A grain of sugar weighs **1.4175×10^{-8}** grams.

This is **315 times** heavier than a speck of dust.

What does a speck of dust weigh ?

Give your answer in standard form.

Answer _____ grams.   [2]

11. a. Calculate $(3\frac{2}{5} - 1\frac{1}{2}) \div (2\frac{1}{4} + 2\frac{1}{2})$

Write your answer in lowest terms.

Answer _____ [2]

b. Insert a pair of brackets into the expression below to give an answer of $\frac{7}{10}$.

$$\frac{1}{4} + \frac{1}{3} \div \frac{5}{12} - \frac{7}{10}$$

[2]

12. An Estate Agent has 2 similar houses to sell.
He bought the first house for £85,000.
He wants to make a profit of 15%.

a. Calculate how much he has to sell the house for to make this profit.

Answer £ _____ [1]

b. He sold the second house for £51,000.
He made a loss on this house of 15%.

Calculate how much he bought this house for.

Answer £ _____ [2]

c. What was the Estate Agent's overall profit or loss ?

Express this profit or loss as a percentage of the total cost of the two houses.
Give your answer to 1 decimal place.

Answer _____% [2]

13. The following fraction calculation is given to two students, Ann and Sam.

"....a third plus a half of three quarters "

Ann writes the sum down as :-

$$\left(\frac{1}{3} + \frac{1}{2}\right) \text{ of } \frac{3}{4}$$

a. Calculate the answer to Ann's sum.

Answer _____ [1]

Sam writes the sum down correctly as :-

$$\frac{1}{3} + \left(\frac{1}{2} \times \frac{3}{4}\right)$$

b. Calculate the answer to Sam's sum.

Answer _____ [1]

c. Calculate the difference between the two answers in its simplest form.

Answer _____ [2]

14. Solve the following inequality writing down all the **integer** solutions.

$$-1 < 2x < 11$$

a. Answer **x** = _____ [1]

b. Write down the largest value of **x** . _____ [1]

15. In an Ice-skating championship two judges, Amy and Claud were awarding marks out of 50 for the competitors.

Below is a scatter graph showing the marks of 7 ice skaters.

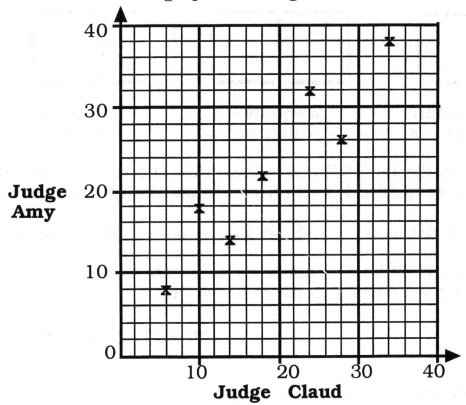

Another skater Harry was awarded a mark of 34 by Claud and 32 by Amy.

a. With an **X** mark Harry's score on the graph. [1]

b. Draw a line of best fit on the scatter graph. [1]

Judge Amy awarded Sara a mark of 24.

c. Using the scatter graph estimate what mark Judge Claud would have awarded Sara.

Answer _____ marks [1]

16. A children's nursery uses straws to make patterns of squares.

The first 3 patterns are shown below.

1 square   2 squares   3 squares
4 straws   7 straws   10 straws

a. From the list of Rules below circle the rule for the number of straws **S**, needed when you know the number of squares, **Q**.

   S = 4Q - 2   S = 2Q + 3   S = 3Q + 1   [2]

b. Use the Rule to calculate the number of straws needed to make 21 squares.

   Answer _____ straws   [1]

c. How many squares can be made with 127 straws ?

   Answer _____ squares   [2]

17. A small lake at a Golf Course has an area of 4000 sq. metres. At the beginning of April in the year 2000, 30% of the lake was covered in Algae weed.

a. What area was covered in Algae weed at the beginning of April ?

   Answer_____ sq. metres   [1]

b. The area of the lake covered by the Algae weed increased in each of the following two months by 10 % of the area of the previous month.
   What area of the lake was covered in Algae weed at the beginning of June ?

   Answer _____ sq. metres   [2]

SHOW ALL YOUR WORKING

18. A Boat race leaves Port P, and travels to Island Q, then to marker buoy R, then to Island S, back to Island Q and returning to Port P. The Boat race begins on a bearing of 110° from Port P to Q. The diagram shows the route of the race.

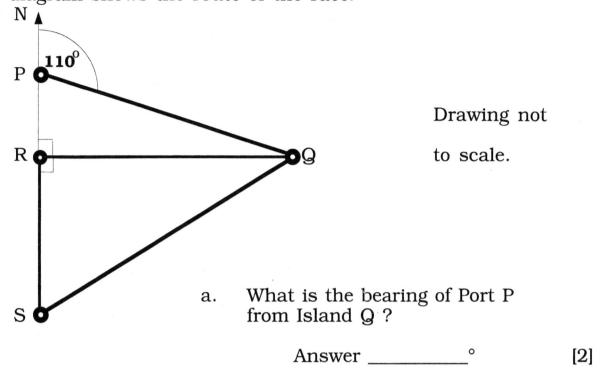

Drawing not

to scale.

a. What is the bearing of Port P from Island Q ?

Answer _____° [2]

b. The Boat race turns at Island Q and travels due west 40 Kms to the buoy R before travelling due south 30 Kms to Island S. Calculate the distance SQ, between Islands S and Q. Give your answer in kilometres.

Answer _____ kms. [1]

c. Calculate the size of angle PQR.

Answer _____° [1]

d. Calculate the distance from Port P to Island Q, to 1 decimal place.

Answer _____ kms. [2]

e. The Boat race returns from Island S through Island Q to Port P. What is the total distance of the race ?

Answer _____ kms. [1]

11.

PTQ Tuition
Practice Materials
Tel: 02879632342

KEY STAGE 3 MATHEMATICS Paper 4/5

PRACTICE TEST 24

Time :
Total time for this test is 1 hour.

Instructions :
Write your name in the space below.
Write your answers in the spaces
provided in the paper.
Check your work carefully.

Information :
Total mark for this Test is 66.
Numbers in brackets at the end of
each question indicate the marks awarded
to each answer or part of an answer.

Mark	
Total	66 (Maximum)

Pupil Name :

_____

1.   Use trial and improvement to solve the following
          equation correct to **1 decimal place**.

$$2x^3 = 99$$

                              Answer **x** = _____   [1]

2.   Enlarge the shape below using a scale factor of $\frac{1}{3}$ and centre C.

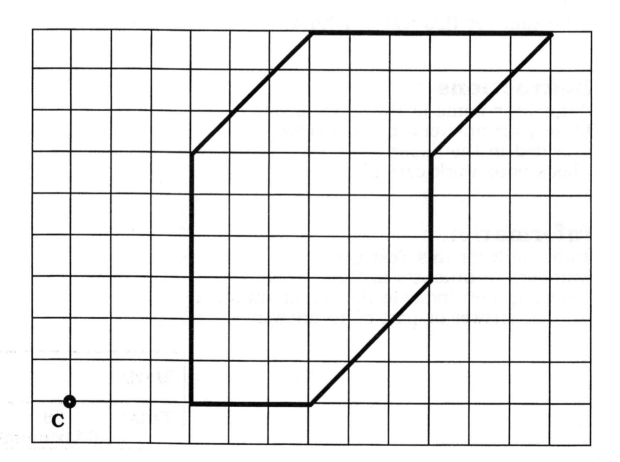

                                                                    [3]

3. The grid below shows two points A and B at the ends of a line.

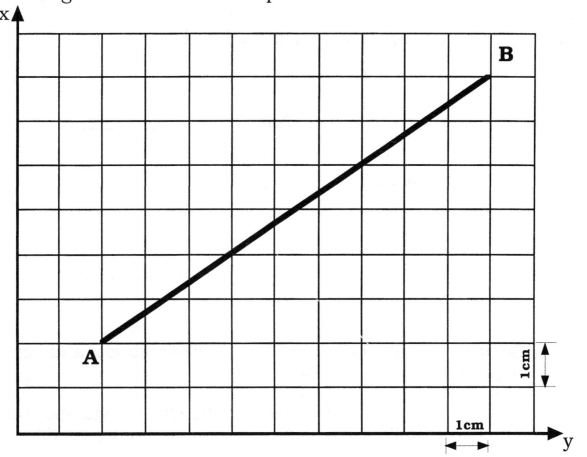

Find the distance from A to B.
give your answer to **2 decimal places.**
Show your working.

Answer   AB = _____ cms   [2]

4. Simplify the following expression.

3y - 6 + (y + 4)(y - 3) - 4

Answer _____   [1]

5.   Solve the following equations :-

a. $2(2x - 3) - 3(x - 2) = 4x$

Answer **x** = _____   [1]

b. $$\frac{2x - 4}{4} = \frac{x + 1}{3}$$

Answer **x** = _____   [2]

6.   Some Christmas cards need a 1st class stamp and some require a 2nd class stamp.

Sara went to the Post Office and bought 63 stamps, some 1st class costing 28p and some 2nd class stamps costing 21p.

She paid a total of £15 . 75 for the stamps.

a.   Using **x** for the 1st class stamps and **y** for the 2nd class stamps write down two equations in **x** and **y** .

_____

_____   [2]

b.   Solve these equations to find the number of 1st and 2nd class stamps.

Answer   1st class stamps _____

2nd class stamps _____   [2]

7.

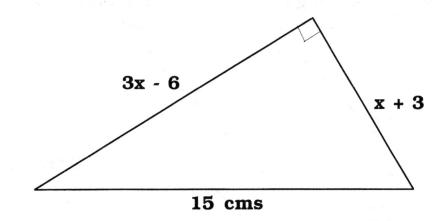

15 cms

a. Using Pythagoras' Theorem for the triangle show that :-

$$x^2 - 3x = 18$$

[2]

b. Use a trial and improvement method to find the value of **x** for which $x^2 - 3x = 18$

Answer **x** = _____ [2]

8. Factorise fully :-

$$10y^2 - 5y$$

Answer _____ [1]

5.

9.   This is a drawing of the tank on the back of a lorry for holding the salt which is spread on icy roads.

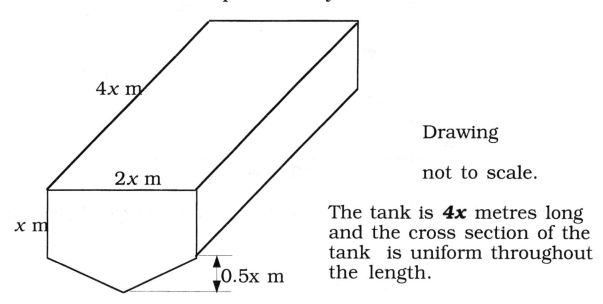

Drawing

not to scale.

The tank is **4x** metres long and the cross section of the tank is uniform throughout the length.

a.   Calculate in terms of **x**, the area of the end of the tank.

Answer _____ square metres   [2]

b.   The total volume of the tank is 24 cubic metres.

Show that $\mathbf{5}x^3 = 12$

[2]

c.   Use a trial and improvement method to find the value of **x**, to one decimal place for which $\mathbf{5}x^3 = 12$.

Answer   **x** = _____metres   [2]

6.

10.   The population of London in 1980
was approximately **7.12 x 10^6**.
By the year 2000 London's population had increased by 20 %.

a.   Write London's population in
2000 in standard form.

Answer _____   [1]

b.   Write this number in full.

Answer _____   [1]

c.   In 1980 the average amount spent on food
per head of population was **£7.8 x 10^2**.

Calculate the total on spent on food
by London's population in 1980.
Give your answer in standard form.

Answer £ _____   [1]

11. a.   Using the formula   **1.5 M + k^2 = h**   calculate **h** when

M = 12, and **k = 6**.

Answer **h** = _____   [1]

b.   Make **k** the subject of the formula.

Answer **k** = _____   [2]

SHOW ALL YOUR WORKING

12. The first 4 terms of a number sequence are shown below.

n	First	Second	Third	Fourth	Fifth	Sixth
	1 x 4	2 x 5	3 x 6	4 x 7		

a. Complete the table showing the fifth and sixth terms. [1]

b. What is the ***n***th term of this sequence ?

Answer ______________________ [2]

c. What is the 50th term of this sequence ?

Answer ______________________ [2]

13. Simplify the following expression, giving your answer in its simplest form.

$$(2s + t)^2 - st$$

Answer ______________________ [2]

14. The drawing is of a Rhombus PQRS.
The diagonal **PR = 76.8 cms** and diagonal **QS = 32 cms.**

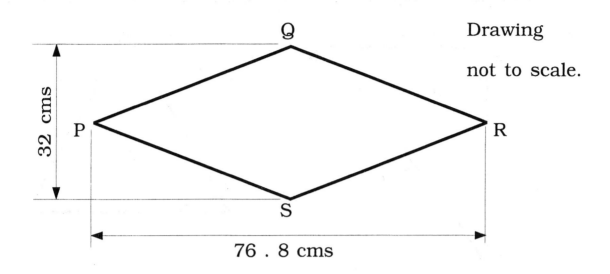

Drawing

not to scale.

a. Calculate the length of PQ.

Answer _____ cms   [2]

b. Calculate the area of the rhombus PQRS.

Answer _____sq. cms.   [2]

15. What is the price, included

VAT at 17.5%, of a TV which

is priced as in the advertisement ?

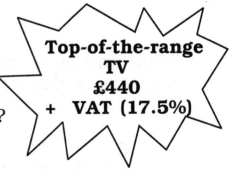

**Top-of-the-range
TV
£440
+ VAT (17.5%)**

Answer £ _____   [2]

16. The triangles shown below, **V** and **W**, have equal perimeters.

Triangle **W** is equilateral. The dimensions are shown in cms.

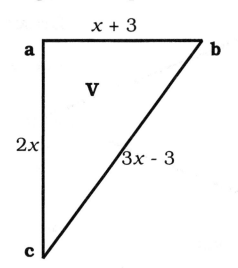
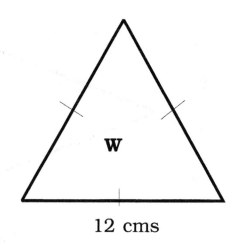

a. Form an equation in terms of **x** and solve it.

Answer : **x** = _____ cms   [1]

b. Using this value of **x** show that triangle **V** is a Right-angled triangle.

[4]

17. What fraction is missing from the box to make this mathematical statement true ?

$$\frac{5}{12} \times \frac{2}{3} = \boxed{} \times \frac{5}{6}$$

Answer _____   [2]

10.

18.   The drawing shows a circular swimming pool at a Spanish holiday resort.
In the Summer holiday season 1% of the water in the pool evaporates over a 24-hour period.

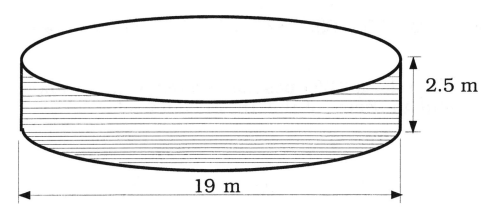

Use 3 . 14 as π.

a.   Calculate the volume of water when the pool was full to the top at the end of June 2001.
Give your answer to 2 decimal places.

Answer _____ cubic metres   [2]

b.   Calculate the volume of water that was in the pool at the end of July 2001.
Give your answer to 2 decimal places.

Answer _____ cubic metres   [4]

19.   **168** expressed as a product of its **prime factors** is **2³ x 3 x 7**.

Given that   **30,240 = 168 x 180** express **30,240** as a product of its **prime factors**, in index form.

Answer **30,240** = _____   [2]

11.

20. 15 'A' levels pupils sat an Economics term test and scored the following marks out of 50.

a. The marks for 13 of the students were as follows :-

29, 32, 35, 35, 37, 38, 39, 40, 40, 40, 42, 43, 45.

Write down TWO possible scores which would have made the median score of the 15 students 39.

Answer _____ [2]

b. 3 of these pupils, Alan, Marus and Sheila then sat a test in Business Studies .

Alan got the smallest marks of x.

The range of the 3 marks was 17.

Sheila got the highest marks.
Write an expression in x for Sheila's marks.

Answer _____ marks [2]

c. The **total** of the three scores was 118 while the **median marks** of 39 was scored by Marus.

Form an equation in x and solve this to find x.

Write down the marks that each pupil received in the Business Studies test.

Answer : Alan _____ marks [1]

Marus _____ marks [1]

Sheila _____ marks [1]

12.

PTQ Tuition
Practice Materials
Tel: 02879632342

KEY STAGE 3 MATHEMATICS Paper 4/5

PRACTICE TEST 25

Time :

Total time for this test is 1 hour.

Instructions :

Write your name in the space below.
Write your answers in the spaces
provided in the paper.
Check your work carefully.

Information :

Total mark for this Test is 66.
Numbers in brackets at the end of
each question indicate the marks awarded
to each answer or part of an answer.

Mark	
Total	66 (Maximum)

Pupil Name :

_____

1. a.   Complete the table below for the function $y = f(x)$.   [2]

x	f(x)
1	2
2.5	8
4	
5.5	20
7	26
8.5	32
10	

   b.   Write down in terms of x, a formula for $f(x)$.

   Answer : $f(x)$ = _____   [2]

   c.   Use the formula for finding the value of $f(13 . 25)$.

   Answer : _____   [2]

2.   Calculate the value of the following :-
      Show your working.

   a. $3^4 + 5^3 - 4^3$

   Answer _____   [1]

   b. $20^2 \div (4^2 + 2^4)$

   Answer _____   [1]

2.

3.   The drawing of the kite below has the following dimensions :-

PT = 8 cms, TS = 10 cms and RT = 24 cms.

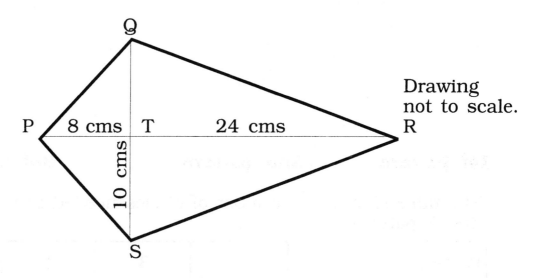

Drawing not to scale.

a.   Calculate the length of QR.

Answer_____ cms.   [2]

b.   Calculate the area of
the kite PQRS.

Answer _____ sq. cms.   [2]

4.   a.   Solve the inequality **x - 2 > -5**

Answer _____   [2]

b.   Given that **x** is an **integer** less than **7** show the solution to
the inequality **x - 2 > -5** on the number line below.
                                                                            [1]

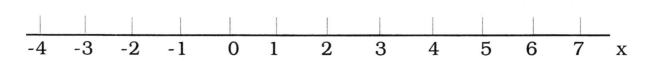

5. The first three patterns of a design are shown below.

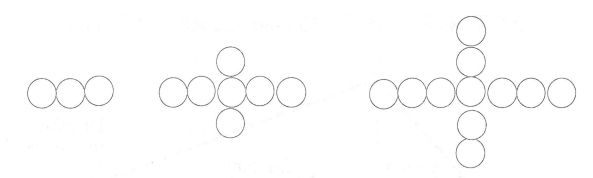

1st pattern   **2nd pattern**   **3rd pattern**

The table shows the number of circles needed to make the first 3 patterns.

Pattern	1	2	3	4	5
No. of circles	3	7	11		

a.   Complete the table showing the number of circles needed for the 4th and 5th patterns.   [1]

b.   Calculate, in terms of **n**, an expression
for the number of circles
needed to make the ' **n** th' pattern.

Answer _____   [2]

c.   The number of circles needed for the **n**th pattern of a **new design** of circles is given by the expression :-

7n + 4

Which pattern in this new design needs **116** circles to create it.

Answer The _____th pattern.   [2]

4.

SHOW ALL YOUR WORKING

6. The spinners shown here are spun once and the numbers that the arrows point towards are recorded.

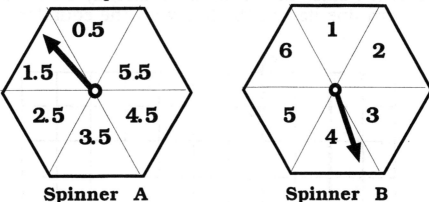

Spinner A   Spinner B

a. Complete the table below to show the score when the two numbers are multiplied. Some are already completed.   [2]

Spinner B

		1	2	3	4	5	6
	0.5	0.5			2.0		
	1.5		3.0			7.5	
Spinner A	2.5			7.5			
	3.5				14		
	4.5		9.0				
	5.5					27.5	

When the numbers to which the arrows pointed in the same spin are multiplied together........

b. What is the probability of scoring more than **20** ? _____ [1]

c. What is the probability of scoring **9** ? _____ [1]

d. What is the probability of getting a score which is a **multiple of 3** ? _____ [1]

e. What is the probability of getting a score which is a **prime number** ? _____ [1]

5.

7. A triangle ABC is to be drawn on the grid below .
Two of the sides lie on the lines already drawn on the grid.
The third line lies on the line with the equation **y = 4 - x.**

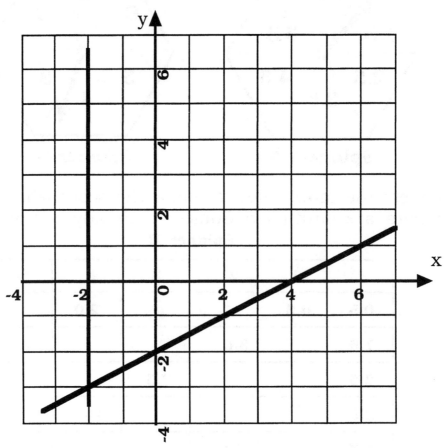

a. Draw the line for the equation **y = 4 - x** on the grid. [2]

b. The co-ordinates of point **B** are (-2,-3).
Point **A** lies on the line **4 = x - 2y.**
Plot all three corners of the triangle, A, B and C.
What are the co-ordinates of A and C ?

A = (____,____) [1]

C = (____,____) [1]

c. The line through B and C has the equation **x = -2.**
The line through A and B has the equation **4 = x - 2y.**

Write down the solution to the
simultaneous equations:-   **x = -2** and **4 = x - 2y.**

Answer :- x = _____ and y = _____ [2]

6.

SHOW ALL YOUR WORKING

8. Concrete is made from Gravel, Sand and Cement in the ratio of **3 : 2 : 1**.

a. If 1000 Kilograms of Sand is used how much Gravel and Cement is needed ?

Answer   Gravel = _____ Kg   [1]

Cement = _____ Kg   [1]

b. At the end of a working day there is 1200 Kilograms of each of the materials, Gravel, Sand and Cement left. What is the maximum amount of Concrete that can be made ?

Answer   _____ Kgs   [2]

9. An example of a function machine is shown below.

IN   **OUT**

x 4   - 4

Writing your answer in its simplest, complete the following .

a.

$\dfrac{3x}{2}$ x 4   - 4

[1]

b.

2 - 2a   x 4   - 4

[1]

c.

x 4   - 4   8 - 8a

[2]

7.

10. The diagram below is of a Patio made up of a quadrant and a rectangle.

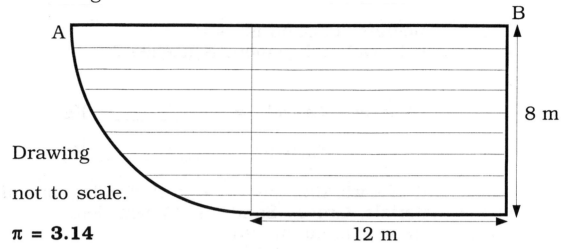

Drawing

not to scale.

$\pi = 3.14$

This patio is covered with wooden decking.

a. Calculate the distance from A to B.

Answer _____ metres [1]

b. To help preserve the wood the decking is treated with a preservative liquid. A one-litre can of the preservative covers 20 square metres.

How many one-litre cans of preservative are needed to treat the decking ?

Answer _____ cans [2]

11. Solve the equation

$$4(x - 3) + 12 = 2(x + 5) - 2$$

Answer **x** = _____ [2]

8.

12.

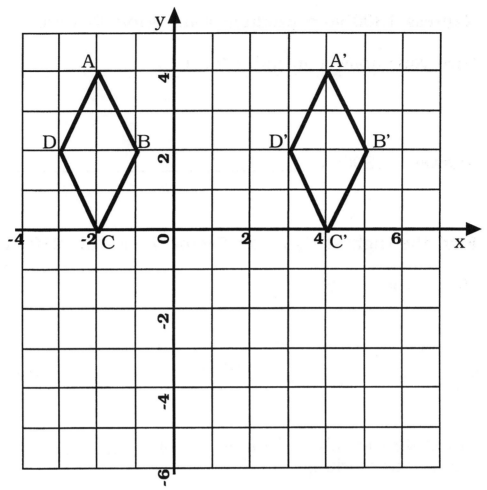

a. Describe fully the single transformation which maps the diamond **A B C D** onto diamond **A' B' C' D'**.

Answer _____

_____ [2]

b. On the grid draw the image of **ABCD** after a rotation of **180°** clockwise about the origin.

Label the diamond **A" B" C" D"**

[2]

13. a. Express 1800 as a product of its prime factors.

Give your answer in index form.

Answer : 1800 = _____ [2]

b. Find the Highest Common Factor (HCF) of 210 and 165.

3   **2**   **2**   **3**

4   **2**   **4**   **4**   Answer _____ [2]

14. Calculate the value of the following :-
Show your working.

a. $(3^3 + 5^2) - (5^2 - 2^3)$

Answer _____ [1]

b. $6^4 \div 4^4 - (3^4 - 2^4)$

Answer _____ [1]

15. The cost of a lawnmower, including VAT at 17.5% is £446.50.

Calculate the price of the lawnmower before VAT is added.

Answer £ _____ [1]

16. The table shows the weights in (Kgs) of 50 Primary school pupils.

Weight (w)	Frequency (f)	
20 - 22	2	
23 - 25	7	
26 - 28	18	
29 - 31	14	
32 - 34	6	
35 - 37	3	

Calculate an estimate of the pupils' mean weight.

Give your answer to 2 decimal places.

Answer w = _____ kgs.   [2]

17. The drawing shows a ramp for wheelchair access.

The Ratio of the length of the ramp to the height is **7 : 2.**

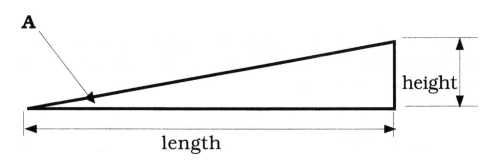

Calculate angle A, giving your answer to 3 significant figures.

Answer :- Angle A = _____°[2]

SHOW ALL YOUR WORKING

18.   At Christmas the 3 children Pam, Max and Sim, in a family were given gifts of money by their parents.

Let £ **y** be the amount that Pam received.

Max received twice as much as Pam and an extra £20.

a.   Write down an expression, in terms of **y**, for the amount of money Max received.

Answer   £ (_____)   [1]

b.   Sim was given half as much as Max.

Write down an expression, in terms of **y**, for the amount of money Sim received.

Answer   £ (_____)   [1]

c.   Show that the total amount of money given by the parents was **4y + 30.**

[2]

d.   If the total amount given by parents was £150, construct an equation in **y** and calculate the amount that each child received.

EQUATION:- _____

Answer   Pam £_____   [1]

Max £_____   [1]

Sim £_____   [1]

12.